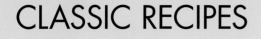

Mexican
cooking

simple
and
delicious
food

Wendy Hobson

Arcturus

ARCTURUS

This edition published in 2013 by Arcturus Publishing Limited
26/27 Bickels Yard, 151–153 Bermondsey Street,
London SE1 3HA

Design copyright ©2013 Arcturus Publishing Limited

ISBN: 978-1-78212-012-4
AD002583US

Printed in China

Contents

Introduction

When we think of Mexican cooking, the first thing that springs to mind must be sunshine and chilies! Vibrant and colorful—in both presentation and tastes—Mexican cooking knows no formality or constraint. It's about having fun with food, enjoying the flavors—throwing a party!

Central to Mexican cooking is the chili. Among the most important crops in the country, this power-packed fruit features in many of Mexico's most famous food exports, beginning with the ubiquitous Carne con Chili that we all love. And the wonderful thing about using chili in our cooking is that we don't have to make our meals as spicy as the Mexicans do. Just go in gently and you can soon begin to spice up your meats a little more if you find you are getting used to the levels of heat. There's no need to take the roof off your mouth if you are not ready for it. But once you are attuned to the chili flavor, I can promise you, it's addictive.

Chili works with all kinds of meat but beef is a Mexican favorite, so there are lots of beef dishes here. But you'll also find chicken and pork, both very popular broiled, sautéed or in a rich stew. Of course, with the sunshine playing such an important role the barbecue won't be far away, and many of these dishes are ideal for outdoor treatment, making them quick and easy for you to cook either al fresco or under your oven broiler.

Rice is, of course, the main accompaniment of choice and that makes meals even easier to put together as rice is simple to cook. However, if you want a change, try some quinoa, a South American grain gaining in popularity because of its delicious nutty taste. Similar to couscous, it goes very well with Mexican dishes.

It wouldn't be Mexican without at least some tortillas, and in this collection, we have included both soft tortillas—ideal for wrapping up your spicy main courses—as well as crispy taco shells. Experiment with the various kinds and see which ones you like best. You will be spoilt for choice even in your local supermarket or store.

Vegetables and pulses, too, are many and varied in Mexican cooking. Beans, peppers, tomatoes, and corn are the favorite local produce. You'll find them cropping up in many recipes. Try to choose colorful vegetables that have ripened under a hot sun to give them the sweetest, juiciest flavors.

With a strong Spanish influence, there are bound to be dishes that are similar to European versions, and that is most noticeable among the desserts. Delicious, slow-cooked Rice Pudding would be at home on any Spanish table. Creamy Crème Caramel, with its fabulous caramelized syrup, also gives you that delightful softness that characterizes Mexican desserts. The contrast makes the whole meal so well balanced—hot and spicy to start, with a perfect smooth and cooling conclusion.

So enjoy this collection of modern Mexican favorites. Serve them for lunch, dinner, or snacks. Enjoy them at home or with company—perhaps with music! Make them subtle or fiery hot. But, above all, serve them with sunshine and panache.

Guacamole

Although this classic dish is available ready-made in the stores, you'll get a far better flavor if you make your own. And you'll know there are no preservatives or stabilizers—just the fresh ingredients packed with nutrients.

Serves 4–6

1 red onion, cut into chunks
1 garlic clove
1 jalapeño pepper, deseeded
1 large bunch of cilantro leaves
Salt and freshly ground black pepper
2 avocados, peeled, pitted, and cut into chunks
Juice of 2 limes

To garnish
Chipotle chips
A few strips of lime zest

1. Put the onion, garlic, pepper, and cilantro in the bowl of a food processor and coarsely chop. Season with salt and pepper.
2. Toss the avocados in the lime juice, add to the food processor and process until the mixture is well blended and still slightly chunky. If you prefer a thinner consistency, simply blend in a little water.
3. Serve garnished with chipotle chips and a few strips of lime zest.

Serves 4

1 tbsp oil
1 onion, chopped
2 garlic cloves, chopped
225g/8oz chicken, cut into chunks
2 tsp chili powder
1 tsp dried oregano
400g/14oz/1 large can chopped tomatoes
2 tbsp tomato paste
450ml/¾pt/2 cups chicken stock
400g/14oz/1 large can black-eyed beans
1 tortilla, cut into short, thin strips (optional)
Salt and freshly ground black pepper
A few parsley leaves

To garnish

A few sage leaves
1 tomato, diced
1 lime, cut into wedges
Tortilla chips

Chicken tortilla soup

This is a chunky soup suitable as a starter or for serving as a main course, accompanied by some more grated cheese or a fresh green salad. Add some boiling water if you want the soup a bit thinner.

1. Heat the oil in a large pan and sauté the onion and garlic over a low heat for several minutes until soft but not browned.
2. Add the chicken and sauté until golden on all sides.
3. Sprinkle in the chili powder and oregano and stir to coat the chicken in the spices.
4. Add the tomatoes, tomato paste, and stock, bring to the boil, then simmer for about 20 minutes until the chicken is tender.
5. Add the black-eyed beans and the strips of tortilla, if liked. Season with a little salt and generously pepper and sprinkle with the parsley. Add a little more stock or water to make the soup as thick or thin as you like it. Simmer gently for about 10 minutes until thoroughly hot.
6. Garnish with the sage and tomato and serve with tortilla chips and lime wedges for guests to squeeze into their soup.

Broiled vegetable enchiladas

These soft corn tortillas can be filled with your favorite vegetables—choose whatever you like—before smothering them in a spicy tomato sauce and topping with golden melted cheese. You can adjust the heat by using less chili. Accompany with a bowl of fresh salad.

Serves 4

1 tbsp oil

1 onion, chopped

2 garlic cloves, chopped

½ jalapeño pepper, seeded and chopped

1 red bell pepper, cut into chunks

2 tsp ground cumin

½ tsp dried oregano

400g/14oz/1 large can chopped or sieved tomatoes

Salt and freshly ground black pepper

225g/8oz vegetables, such as sweet potatoes, carrots or zucchini, or vegetables of your choice, cut into chunks

4–8 corn tortillas

100g/4oz Monterey Jack cheese, grated

To serve

Tomatoes

Lettuce or salad leaves

1. Heat the oil in a skillet and sauté the onion for a few minutes over a low heat until soft but not browned.
2. Add the garlic and both peppers and sauté for 2 minutes.
3. Add the cumin and oregano and stir into the mixture, then add the tomatoes and season with salt and pepper. Simmer for about 30 minutes, or preferably longer, until the sauce is thick and rich.
4. Add the vegetables and continue to cook until they are just tender but still with a bit of crunch. How long you cook them will depend on the vegetables you choose, but allow about 10 minutes.
5. Heat the broiler.
6. Reserve a few spoonfuls of the tomato sauce, then spoon some of the tomato and vegetable mixture on to a tortilla, roll it up and place in a flameproof dish. Repeat with all the remaining tortillas. Spoon the reserved tomato sauce over the top and sprinkle with the cheese.
7. Broil for a few minutes until the cheese is bubbling and the whole dish is heated through.
8. Serve with tomatoes and the salad.

Serves 4

1 tbsp oil

1 onion, chopped

1 garlic clove, chopped

1 jalapeño pepper, deseeded and chopped

2 tbsp chopped cilantro

1 tsp dried oregano

1 bay leaf

1 tsp chili powder (optional)

900ml/1¾pt/3¾ cups beef, chicken or vegetable stock

400g/14oz/1 large can sieved tomatoes

400g/14oz/1 large can red kidney beans, drained

400g/14oz/1 large can black-eyed beans, drained

Salt and freshly ground black pepper

Bean and vegetable stew

Beans are a popular element of Mexican food, and this dish combines black-eyed and red kidney beans in a tasty stock. If you use dried beans, soak them overnight in cold water, then boil rapidly for 15 minutes before simmering for an hour.

1. Heat the oil in a large pan and sauté the onion, garlic, and pepper gently for a few minutes until soft but not browned.
2. Add the herbs and stir well. Add the extra chili powder if you like a hot dish.
3. Stir in the stock and bring to the boil.
4. Stir in the tomatoes and beans, bring to a gentle simmer and simmer for about 20 minutes until the broth has reduced slightly and the beans are soft.
5. Season with salt and pepper and serve in deep bowls.

Fresh fish tacos

Serves 4

1 lime
2 salmon steaks
150ml/¼pt/⅔ cup milk or fish stock
1 mango, peeled, pitted, and sliced
1 red bell pepper, sliced
1 red onion, sliced
4 tomatoes, sliced
1 avocado
A handful of lettuce leaves, shredded
6–8 taco shells
A few cilantro leaves

For the fresh tomato salsa
4 tomatoes
½ jalapeño pepper, seeded
and finely chopped
1 red onion, finely chopped
1 garlic clove, finely chopped
1 tbsp finely chopped cilantro
A pinch of sugar
Salt and freshly ground black pepper

To serve
Guacamole (page 7) (optional)
Sour cream (optional)

Pile this delicious filling into crisp taco shells and treat yourself by making some home-made guacamole or tomato salsa to serve with it. You could also use the same filling for wheat or corn tortilla. This quantity will make a light lunch or starter.

1. Cut the lime in half. Cut one half into wedges and squeeze the juice from the other half.
2. Start the tomato salsa by dicing the tomatoes, discarding the seeds if you prefer. Place in a colander to drain.
3. Put the salmon in a small pan, cover with the milk or stock, then bring to a simmer and heat gently for about 10 minutes until the fish is cooked and flakes easily.
4. Strain and leave to cool, then flake into bite-sized chunks.
5. Transfer the salsa tomatoes to a bowl and mix in the jalapeño pepper, onion, garlic, and cilantro. Sprinkle with the sugar and a splash of the lime juice, and season with salt and pepper to taste. Spoon into a serving bowl.
6. Once the fish is cool, place it in a bowl and add the mango, pepper, onion, and tomatoes. Use your hands to toss the ingredients together gently.
7. Peel, pit, and slice the avocado and toss in lime juice to prevent discoloration, then add to the salad in the bowl.
8. Spoon the mixture into the tacos and garnish with lime wedges and cilantro leaves. Serve the salsa separately for people to add their own to their tacos. You may also like to serve sour cream and guacamole on the side.

Chicken and avocado wraps

Wraps make great lunchbox food and are ideal for picnics—the perfect portable food, with a tasty filling encased in a soft tortilla. This recipe will make about four wraps, but you can use either more or less filling to suit your own appetite.

Serves 4

2 chicken breasts
300ml/½pt/1¼ cups chicken stock
2 tomatoes, chopped
1 avocado
A squeeze of lime or lemon juice
120ml/4fl oz/½ cup sour cream
A dash of chili sauce
Salt and freshly ground black pepper
4 large soft corn tortillas
A handful of mixed salad leaves

1. Put the chicken in a pan, cover with the stock and bring to a simmer. Simmer gently for about 15–20 minutes until the chicken is cooked through and no longer runs pink when pierced.
2. Leave to cool in the stock, then remove and drain the chicken, reserving the stock.
3. Cut the chicken into thin strips, place in a bowl, and add the tomatoes.
4. Peel and pit the avocado and cut into strips. Toss in a generous squeeze of lime or lemon juice, then add to the bowl and toss together.
5. Add the sour cream and a dash of chili sauce to taste, and season with salt and pepper. Mix everything together so the chicken and avocado are moist and coated in the tomato juice and sour cream.
6. Divide the filling among the tortillas. Start rolling up the tortillas, folding in one side as you do so to keep the filling inside.
7. Serve on a bed of salad leaves.

Broiled chicken with quinoa and vegetables

A healthy option for lunch or dinner, quinoa is a delicious grain with a nutty flavor that goes beautifully with chicken. Simply cooked and served with a fresh salad, this is a dish for everyone to enjoy.

Serves 4

4 chicken breasts
15g/½oz/1 tbsp butter, melted
A pinch of chili powder
Salt and freshly ground black pepper
350g/12oz/1¾ cups quinoa
900ml/1½pt/3¾ cups chicken or
  vegetable stock
225g/8oz cherry tomatoes
A few basil leaves, torn into shreds

For the salad
A handful of basil leaves
50g/2oz/½ cup whole almonds
8 cherry tomatoes, halved
2 carrots, grated
50g/2oz/½ cup grated cheese
1 tbsp olive oil
A pinch of chili powder

1. Heat the broiler to medium.
2. Brush the chicken with the butter and season with chili, and salt, and pepper.
3. Grill the chicken for 10 minutes until it is browned, turning once, then reduce to medium-low and continue to cook for about 15–20 minutes until the chicken juices run clear when pierced with a knife.
4. Meanwhile, put the quinoa in a pan and pour in the stock. Bring to the boil, then simmer gently for about 20 minutes until tender and the water has been absorbed. Season with salt and pepper.
5. Stir in the tomatoes and basil. Check and adjust the seasoning to taste.
6. To make the salad, mix together all the ingredients, drizzle with the oil and sprinkle with paprika.
7. Spoon the quinoa on to serving plates, top with the chicken and serve the salad on the side.

Pepper and lime roast chicken

You can use a whole chicken for this recipe, or even chicken portions if you reduce the cooking time. Alternatively, use a turkey crown and cook for longer—the pack will give you cooking times. You can buy boned chicken ready-prepared at the store.

Serves 4

450g/1lb waxy potatoes, halved
Salt and freshly ground black pepper
3 tbsp oil
1 tsp paprika
1 boned chicken
1 red bell pepper, cut into chunks
4 kumquats, thickly sliced
8 cherry tomatoes
2 tbsp chopped parsley
1 lime, sliced and quartered
A handful of thyme leaves
A few fresh basil leaves

1. Heat the oven to 200°C/400°F/Gas 6.
2. Put the potatoes in a pan, cover with lightly salted water, and bring to the boil. Simmer for 3 minutes, then drain well.
3. Meanwhile, heat the oil in a Dutch oven large enough to take all the ingredients. Season the chicken with paprika, salt, and pepper, put the chicken in the Dutch oven and turn to coat in the hot oil. Put in the oven for 30 minutes until the chicken is browned.
4. Add the pepper, kumquats, and tomatoes, stir around, then add the parsley and lime. Reduce the oven temperature to 180°C/350°F/Gas 4 and return the dish to the oven for a further 45–60 minutes until the chicken is cooked through and browned and the fruit and vegetables are tender, stirring at least once.
5. Sprinkle with the thyme, and garnish with the basil leaves to serve.

Serves 4

For the seasoning mix
1 tbsp cornstarch
2 tsp chili powder
1 tsp sugar
1 tsp paprika
1 tsp salt
½ tsp onion powder
A pinch of garlic powder
A pinch of ground cumin
A pinch of cayenne pepper

For the chicken
2 tbsp oil
2 red onions, sliced
1 red bell pepper, cut into strips
1 green bell pepper, cut into strips
2 garlic cloves, chopped
450g/1lb chicken breasts, cut into strips
250ml/8fl oz/1 cup water
8 flour tortillas

To serve
Guacamole (page 7)
Sour cream
Tomato salsa (page 11)

Chicken fajitas

This is one of my favorite recipes and makes a delicious meal. You can buy a ready-made fajitas seasoning mix, which is great for when you are busy, but it's fun to make your own. Store it in an airtight jar in the fridge and use with meat or fish.

1. Combine all the ingredients for the seasoning mix. You will need 2 tbsp for this recipe; store the remainder in an airtight jar for up to a month. Alternatively, use a sachet of ready-made fajita spice mix
2. Heat the oil in a large skillet and sauté the onions, peppers, and garlic for 5 minutes over a low heat until soft but not browned.
3. Add the chicken, raise the heat to medium and sauté until just browned.

4. Sprinkle with 2 tbsp of the fajita seasoning mix and stir in well. Cook for 5 minutes.
5. Add the water and continue to cook for about 10 minutes until the chicken is cooked, most of the liquid has evaporated and the ingredients are coated in the spicy sauce.
6. Serve with the tortillas, with bowls of guacamole, sour cream, and tomato salsa on the side. To eat, place spoonfuls of chicken and sauces on a tortilla and roll up.

Spiced beef empanada

These parcels of yeast pastry are filled with a spicy beef mixture. They make a tasty meal served with salad or can be served as a snack on their own, and are delicious either hot or cold.

Serves 4

For the filling

1 tbsp oil

1 onion, chopped

2 garlic cloves, crushed

1 jalapeño pepper, seeded and chopped

450g/1lb lean beef, diced

2 tbsp lime juice

1 tsp dried oregano

1 tsp ground cumin

½ tsp ground coriander

A pinch of chili powder

Salt and freshly ground black pepper

For the yeast pastry

450g/1lb all-purpose flour, plus more for dusting

1 tbsp/1 sachet instant yeast

2 tsp sugar

A pinch of salt

1 egg

200ml/7fl oz/scant 1 cup warm milk, plus extra for brushing

1. Heat the oil in a skillet and sauté the onion, garlic, and pepper for a few minutes over a low heat until soft but not browned.
2. Raise the heat, add the beef, and sauté until browned. Stir in the lime juice and spices, and season with salt and pepper. Add a little boiling water and stir everything together. Cover and simmer for about 30 minutes until the beef is tender. Leave to cool to room temperature.
3. Meanwhile, to make the pastry, mix the flour, yeast, sugar, and salt in a food processor or mixer fitted with the dough hook. Add the egg and gradually add enough of the milk to make the mixture bind into a soft dough. Continue to process for 5 minutes until you have a smooth and non-sticky dough. Transfer to an oiled bowl, cover with oiled plastic wrap and leave in a warm place for 30 minutes until doubled in size.
4. Heat the oven to 200°C/400°F/Gas 6 and put a greased cookie sheet in the oven to heat.
5. Punch down the dough on a lightly floured surface, then roll out and cut into 20cm/8in rounds.
6. Spoon the filling on to half of each of the pastry rounds, moisten the edges, then fold in half and seal together, crimping the edges to seal them. Brush with milk and place the empanadas on the prepared sheet.
7. Bake in the oven for about 15–20 minutes until golden brown.

Beef tacos

I like to make tacos with ground beef, but in Mexico they use chunks of beef. Both options work well, so take your choice. You can make them as hot as you like by using more or fewer peppers.

Serves 4

1 tbsp oil
1 onion, sliced
1 garlic clove, chopped
1 green bell pepper, chopped
1 jalapeño pepper, seeded and chopped
500g/1lb 2oz ground beef
150ml/¼pt/⅔ cup sieved tomatoes
2 tbsp tomato paste
1 lime, sliced
Salt and freshly ground black pepper
8 taco shells
a handful of lettuce leaves, torn into pieces
2 tomatoes, chopped
50g/2oz/½ cup grated strong cheese

To serve
Guacamole (page 7)
1 gherkin, sliced

1. Heat the oil in a heavy-based pan and sauté the onion, garlic, and both the peppers over a low heat for about 5 minutes until soft but not browned.
2. Increase the heat, add the beef, and stir until browned and the grains are separate.
3. Add the tomatoes, tomato paste, and a squeeze of lime juice. Season with salt and pepper. Bring to the boil, then reduce the heat, partially cover, and simmer for about 40 minutes until the meat is tender and the sauce is thick. Add a little boiling water if it seems too thick, or remove the lid to let it reduce if it's too thin.
4. Heat the oven to 170°C/325°F/Gas 3.
5. Warm the tacos in the oven for a few minutes, then arrange on a serving plate.
6. Taste the sauce and adjust the seasoning if necessary. Spoon the meat into the taco shells with some lettuce and chopped tomatoes, then sprinkle with the cheese. Garnish with the lime slices and serve with the guacamole and gherkin.

Beef burritos

This combines the traditional flavors of Mexico, with tomato, peppers, and spiced beans. The avocado provides a pleasant contrast to the heat of the chilis. You could use a spoonful of guacamole or sour cream instead, if you like.

Serves 4

2 tbsp oil
1 onion, chopped
2 garlic cloves, chopped
450g/1lb ground beef
1 tsp ground cumin
2 tsp chili powder
120ml/4fl oz/½ cup sieved tomatoes
2 tbsp tomato paste
400g/14oz/1 large can refried beans
120ml/4fl oz/½ cup beef stock, or more to taste
4–6 soft flour tortillas
4 tomatoes, cut into wedges
A handful of lettuce leaves
1 avocado, peeled, pitted, and chopped
a squeeze of lime juice

1. Heat the oil in a pan and sauté the onion and garlic for a few minutes over a low heat until softened but not colored.
2. Add the beef and sauté until browned.
3. Stir in the cumin and chili, then the sieved tomatoes and tomato paste, and cook for a few minutes until well mixed.
4. Add the refried beans and stock, cover, and simmer gently for about 20 minutes until thoroughly hot, with a thick sauce.
5. Heat the oven to 170°C/325°F/Gas 3.
6. Warm the tortillas in the oven for a few minutes, or in the microwave for a few seconds, until heated through but still soft.
7. Spoon the meat mixture into the tortillas, top with some lettuce and tomatoes, and scatter with avocado. Squeeze over a little lime juice, roll up and serve.

Beef tamales with tomato salsa

To make the tamales you create a soft dough to encase the meat filling, then wrap the whole tamales in corn husks to steam them. It takes a little longer than some recipes but it's well worth it.

Serves 4

3 tbsp oil
1 onion, chopped
2 garlic cloves, chopped
450g/1lb chuck steak, diced
375ml/13fl oz/1½ cups beef stock
Salt and freshly ground black pepper
1 tbsp all-purpose flour
2 tsp chili powder
8 dried corn husks

For the tomato salsa

4 tomatoes, finely chopped
1 green chili, seeded and finely chopped
1 small onion, finely chopped
1 tbsp chopped cilantro leaves
Juice of ½ lime
Salt and freshly ground black pepper

For the dough

300g/11oz/3 cups masa harina or all-purpose flour
15g/½ oz/1 tbsp butter, melted
3 tbsp oil
250ml/8fl oz/1 cup beef stock

1. Heat the oven to 180°C/350°F/Gas 4.
2. Heat 1 tbsp of the oil in a large Dutch oven and sauté the onion and garlic over a low heat for about 5 minutes until soft but not browned.
3. Add the beef, raise the heat to high, and sauté for a further 5 minutes until browned on all sides.
4. Add 250ml/8fl oz/1 cup of the stock and season with salt and pepper. Cover and cook in the oven for about 1 hour until the meat is tender.
5. Remove the meat from the dish with a slotted spoon and shred finely.
6. Drain off the cooking liquid and make up to 250ml/8fl oz/1 cup with some of the remaining stock or a little water.
7. Add 1 tbsp oil to the Dutch oven and place over a medium heat. Add the beef, sprinkle with the flour and chili powder, and cook for 1 minute, stirring continuously.
8. Stir in the cooking liquid until well blended and cook for 5 minutes. Leave to cool to room temperature.
9. Put the corn husks in a bowl of water and weigh them down so they stay beneath the surface. Soak for 30 minutes.
10. To make the salsa, simply mix all the ingredients together in a food processor or by hand.
11. Put the masa harina or all-purpose flour in a bowl with a pinch of salt and add the butter and oil. Gradually stir in the stock to make a soft dough, adding a little extra water if necessary.
12. Drain the soaked corn husks and pull off a few strips to use to tie the tamales. Spread one husk out on the work surface. Take a piece of the dough and press and roll it out on the first husk

to a 10 x 7.5cm/4 x 3in rectangle. Put a spoonful of the beef on the dough and roll up, tucking in the ends. Roll the husk around the outside of the dough and tie with strip of husk. Repeat with the remaining tamales.

13. Stand the tamales upright in a vegetable steamer and steam for about 45 minutes until the dough is firm. Remove from the steamer and leave to stand in a warm place for a few minutes before serving with the tomato salsa.

Serves 4

3 tbsp oil

1 onion, chopped

2 garlic cloves, chopped

1 red bell pepper, chopped

1 jalapeño pepper, seeded and chopped

450g/1lb ground beef

2 tsp chili (optional)

120ml/4fl oz/½ cup red wine

800g/1lb 10oz/2 large cans chopped tomatoes

250ml/8fl oz/1 cup sieved tomatoes

400g/14oz/1 large can red kidney beans, rinsed and drained

Salt and freshly ground black pepper

75g/3oz/¾ cup grated cheese

A few chives

A dill sprig

To serve

Chipotle chips

Tomatoes and a mixed salad

Carne con chili

This must be the best known of all Mexican dishes and is surely the most popular. A really versatile dish, it can be served with tacos, tortilla, rice or, as we have here, with chipotle chips and salad. Try it with the tomato salsa on page 11, too.

1. Heat the oil in a large pan over a medium heat and sauté the onion, garlic, and peppers for 5 minutes until soft but not browned.
2. Stir in the beef and cook over a high heat for 5 minutes, stirring to break up and brown the meat.
3. Stir in the chili powder, if using. Stir in the wine and cook for 3 minutes.
4. Add the tomatoes and sieved tomatoes and bring to the boil. Reduce the heat and simmer gently for 30 minutes until the sauce is thick. Cook it for longer if you wish, covering the pan if the sauce is thickening too much.
5. Add the kidney beans and cook for 15 minutes until everything is heated through and well blended. Season with salt and pepper.
6. Sprinkle with the cheese, garnish with the herbs, and serve with chipotle chips and salad.

Pork topped with onions

Sometimes the simplest dishes are the most effective, and this is a lovely dish of red onions and lightly caramelized pork chops served on a fresh bed of salad leaves and ripe tomatoes.

1. Heat the broiler to medium.
2. Brush the pork chops with a little of the oil and sprinkle with half the oregano and chili, choosing whether you want it more or less spicy. Broil for about 20 minutes until cooked through and lightly browned, turning occasionally.
3. Meanwhile, heat the remaining oil in a skillet and sauté the onions over a medium heat until soft but not browned. Stir in the sugar with the remaining oregano and chili and continue to cook for about 20 minutes until lightly caramelized.
4. Serve the chops on a bed of salad leaves, topped with the onions and garnished with the rosemary.

Serves 4

4 pork chops
2 tbsp oil
1–2 tsp dried oregano
1–2 tsp chili powder
4 red onions, thinly sliced
1 tsp sugar
A few rosemary sprigs

To serve
6 tomatoes, cut into wedges
Mixed salad leaves

Pork with mole sauce

Cooking savory dishes with chocolate has been popular in Mexico since before the Mayans. It is a surprisingly effective combination, rich and delicious, perfectly complementing the flavor and texture of the pork.

Serves 4

4 pork cutlets or lean pork meat, cut into chunks
Salt and freshly ground black pepper
A pinch of ground cinnamon
A pinch of ground cumin
A pinch of dried oregano
1 tbsp oil

For the mole sauce
1 tbsp oil
1 onion, finely chopped
1 garlic clove, chopped
1 dried red chilli, seeded and crushed
1 tsp ground coriander
½ tsp ground cinnamon
½ tsp ground cloves
1 tbsp chopped cilantro
600ml/1pt/2½ cups chicken or vegetable stock
2 tbsp tomato paste
50g/2oz unsweetened chocolate, chopped
1 tbsp lime juice
4 tbsp water

To serve
A few cilantro sprigs
1 onion, sliced into rings
2 radishes, sliced
Boiled rice garnished with mango

1. Season the pork with salt and pepper, then sprinkle with the cinnamon, cumin, and oregano.

2. Heat the oil in a skillet and sauté the pork over a medium heat until lightly browned, then reduce the heat and cook gently for about 20 minutes until cooked to your liking.

3. Meanwhile, heat the oil for the sauce in a separate pan and sauté the onion and garlic for 2 minutes over a medium heat until soft but not browned. Add the spices and herbs, then stir in the stock and tomato paste and bring to the boil. Simmer for 10 minutes, stirring occasionally.

4. Purée with a hand blender or in a blender, adding the chocolate, lime juice, and water. Return to the pan and heat gently, partially covered, for about 20 minutes, adding a little boiling water if the sauce becomes too thick. Season with salt and pepper.

5. Pour the sauce over the pork, garnish with cilantro, onion, and radishes then serve with boiled rice, garnished with a few cubes of mango.

Serves 4

1 tbsp oil

900g/2lb pork shoulder, cut
into chunks

2 garlic cloves, chopped

A pinch of ground cumin

1 cinnamon stick

1 bay leaf

Salt and freshly ground black pepper

about 250ml/8fl oz/1 cup water

400g/14oz/1 large can
refried beans

50g/2oz/½ cup grated cheese

A few parsley sprigs

To serve

Corn tortillas

1 lime, cut into wedges

Guacamole (page 7)

Tomato salsa (page 11)

1 carrot, grated

Tender fried pork

Guacamole is the best accompaniment for this, a delicious pork dish, often served with refried beans and Spanish rice, and topped with lots of grated cheese. The pork needs long, slow cooking but requires no attention while it is in the oven.

1. Heat the oven to 180°C/350°F/Gas 4.
2. Heat the oil in a large Dutch oven over a high heat, add the pork and sauté for 5 minutes until browned.
3. Stir in the garlic and cumin, add the cinnamon and bay leaf and season with salt and pepper. Add enough water to come halfway up the pork.
4. Cover and cook in the oven for about 2 hours, stirring occasionally, until the pork is beginning to fall apart and most of the liquid has evaporated.

5. Lift the pork out of the pan with a slotted spoon and shred the meat. Return it to the pan, then put back in the oven for a further 30 minutes or so until the pork is caramelized.
6. Warm the tortillas in the oven for the last few minutes of cooking. Heat the refried beans in a pan until hot.
7. Spoon the pork on to the tortillas, sprinkle with cheese, and garnish with parsley. Serve with the refried beans, lime, guacamole, tomato salsa, and grated carrot.

Spanish rice

This is the ideal dish to accompany your Mexican main courses, or you could add some cooked chicken or prawns and make it a meal in itself, perhaps served with some tortilla or a fresh salad.

Serves 4

1 tbsp oil

1 garlic clove, crushed

50g/2oz mushrooms, chopped

1 zucchini, chopped

1 red bell pepper, cut into strips

300g/10oz/3 cups long-grain rice

1 tsp chili powder

1 tsp dried oregano

½ tsp ground cumin

200g/7oz/1 small can chopped tomatoes

450ml/¾pt/2 cups chicken stock

Salt and freshly ground black pepper

100g/4oz green beans, cut into chunks

A handful of frozen peas

1. Heat the oil in a large wok or skillet over a medium heat and sauté the garlic, mushrooms, zucchini, and pepper for 4 minutes.
2. Add the rice and stir well, then stir in the chili, oregano, and cumin. Add the tomatoes and stock and bring to the boil. Season with salt and pepper. Cover and simmer for about 7 minutes.
3. Add the beans and peas, return to a simmer and cook for a few more minutes until the rice is tender and the water has been absorbed. Stir well before serving.

Crème caramel

Serves 4

125g/4½oz/generous 1 cup
superfine sugar
150ml/¼pt/⅔ cup water
4 eggs
600ml/1pt/2½ cups milk

This modest little dessert is so easy to make but is always delicious, especially when it follows a spicy Mexican meal. The cool flavor and smooth texture make the ideal conclusion to a robust main course.

1. Reserve 2 tbsp of the sugar and put the remainder in a heavy-based pan with the water. Dissolve the sugar slowly over a low heat, stirring occasionally.
2. Bring to the boil and boil gently for about 5 minutes, without stirring, until it turns a rich golden brown.
3. Remove from the heat immediately and pour into a 15cm/6in soufflé dish or divide among individual molds. Leave to cool.
4. Heat the oven to 170°C/325°F/Gas 3.
5. Lightly beat the eggs in a bowl and add the reserved sugar.
6. Warm the milk, then pour it on to the eggs, whisking continuously. Strain over the cooled caramel.
7. Place the molds in a baking pan and fill with water to come 2.5cm/1in up the side of the molds. Bake in the oven for 1 hour until set.
8. Leave to set in the molds, preferably overnight in the fridge, then turn out onto plates to serve.

This light sponge cake is soaked in evaporated milk, condensed milk, and heavy cream—hence the Mexican name *très leches*. You can use the leftover milk to make a Mexican Rice Pudding (page 30).

Serves 4

100g/4oz/1 cup all-purpose flour
1½ tsp baking powder
A pinch of salt
5 eggs, separated
225g/8oz/1 cup superfine sugar
75ml/3fl oz/⅓ cup milk
1 tsp vanilla extract
400g/14oz/1 can sweetened
   condensed milk
400/14oz/1 can evaporated milk
60ml/2fl oz/¼ cup heavy cream
600ml/1pt/2½ cups whipped cream
   (optional)

Three-milk cake

1. Heat the oven to 180°C/350°F/Gas 4. Grease and line a 33 x 23cm/13 x 9in baking pan.
2. Mix the flour, baking powder, and salt in a large bowl.
3. Beat the egg yolks with 175g/6oz/¾ cup of the sugar until pale and doubled in volume. Add the milk and vanilla and stir together very gently.
4. Gently stir the egg yolk mixture into the flour.
5. Beat the egg whites until they form soft peaks. Still beating, pour in the remaining sugar and continue to beat until the whites are stiff but not dry. Fold the egg whites into the cake mixture. Pour into the prepared pan and level the top.
6. Bake in the oven for 35–45 minutes until risen and spongy and a knife inserted into the center comes out clean.
7. Turn out on to a deep dish and leave to cool completely.
8. Meanwhile, mix the condensed milk, evaporated milk, and cream in a jug, then remove 300ml/½pt/1¼ cups which you will not need.
9. Prick the cake all over with a fork. Slowly spoon the milk over the cake, making sure you pour it evenly all over. Leave to stand for about 30 minutes to absorb the liquid.
10. Whip the cream until stiff, if using, then spread over the top of the cake, and sides if you wish, piping some decorations on the top.

Mexican rice pudding

This cinnamon-spiced rice pudding will make a luscious end to a meal. If you have mixed milk left over from the Three-milk Cake (page 29), make it up to 375ml/13fl oz/1½ cups with milk and use it instead of either the evaporated or condensed milk.

Serves 4

225g/8oz/1 cup pudding rice
1 cinnamon stick
400g/14oz/1 large can evaporated milk
400g/14oz/1 large can sweetened condensed milk
250ml/8fl oz/1 cup whole milk
1 tsp finely grated lemon zest

To decorate
A pinch of ground cinnamon
A few strips of lemon zest

1. Put the rice in a heavy-based pan, add the cinnamon stick, and just cover with cold water. Bring to the boil, then simmer for about 15–20 minutes until the rice is tender.
2. Strain well. Reserve a little of the cinnamon for decoration.
3. Return the rice to the pan and add the three milks and the lemon zest. Bring to the boil, then reduce the heat and simmer, stirring continuously, for about 20 minutes until the rice is thick and creamy.
4. Dust with ground cinnamon and garnish with a few pieces of the cinnamon stick and the lemon zest to serve.